Lerner SPORTS

G.O.A.T.

MEN'S BASKETBALL TEAMS

MATT DOEDEN

Lerner Publications ◆ M

Lerner Publications Company
An imprint of Lerner Publishing Group, Inc.
241 First Avenue North
Minneapolis, MN 55401 USA

For reading levels and more information, look up this title at www.lernerbooks.com.

Main body text set in Aptifer Sans LT Pro. Typeface provided by Linotype AG.

Editor: Shee Yang **Designer:** Kimberly Morales

Library of Congress Cataloging-in-Publication Data

Names: Doeden, Matt, author.
Title: G.O.A.T. men's basketball teams / Matt Doeden.
Description: Minneapolis : Lerner Publications, [2021] | Series: Greatest of all time teams (Lerner sports) |
   Includes bibliographical references and index. | Audience: Ages 7–11 | Audience: Grades 2–3 | Summary:
   "Does having Kobe Bryant on the roster make a team great? Or does the number of championships carry
   more weight? Backed up with facts and stats, follow along to find out who makes the cut!"— Provided by
   publisher.
Identifiers: LCCN 2020009623 (print) | LCCN 2020009624 (ebook) | ISBN 9781728404431 (library binding) |
   ISBN 9781728418254 (ebook)
Subjects: LCSH: Basketball teams—United States—Juvenile literature. | Basketball—United States—Juvenile
   literature.
Classification: LCC GV885.1 .D634 2021 (print) | LCC GV885.1 (ebook) | DDC 796.323—dc23

LC record available at https://lccn.loc.gov/2020009623
LC ebook record available at https://lccn.loc.gov/2020009624

Manufactured in the United States of America
1-48501-49015-7/30/2020

TABLE OF CONTENTS

Michael Jordan secures a rebound against the Charlotte Hornets.

SWISH!

Basketball is one of the world's most popular sports. For decades, basketball superstars like LeBron James, Michael Jordan, and Bill Russell have made millions of people fall in love with the sport. They've led some of the greatest of all time (G.O.A.T.) teams in basketball.

FACTS AT A GLANCE

>> The Boston Celtics won eight National Basketball Association (NBA) championships in a row from 1959–1966.

>> The 2015–2016 Golden State Warriors won their first 24 games on their way to an NBA-best 73–9 season.

>> In the 2016–2017 season, the Warriors went 16–1 in the postseason to win their second NBA title in three years. It's the greatest playoff run in NBA history.

>> The 1995–1996 Chicago Bulls went 72–10 on their way to the title. It's the best record ever from an NBA champion.

>> The 1992 US Olympic team had 11 future Hall of Famers.

But it's not just superstars that make a team great. Teams win and lose based on how well they work together. They need pinpoint passing, strong defense, and clutch shooting to become the best.

Since the NBA formed in 1949, it has featured the greatest talent and teams in the world. Teams battle each spring in the NBA playoffs to advance to the NBA Finals. Each season the Finals crown a new champion.

Dahntay Jones goes up against Paul Pierce for a dunk.

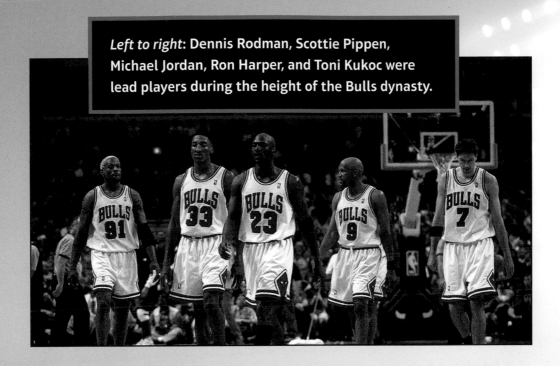

Left to right: Dennis Rodman, Scottie Pippen, Michael Jordan, Ron Harper, and Toni Kukoc were lead players during the height of the Bulls dynasty.

The game has changed a lot over the years. But one thing has remained the same: dynasties rule the NBA. From the 1950s Los Angeles Lakers to the 1960s Boston Celtics, the 1990s Chicago Bulls to Steph Curry's reign with the Golden State Warriors, superstars have joined forces to dominate the league.

The 2015–2016 Golden State Warriors had the best regular season in NBA history. They won 73 games—more than any other team. But they didn't win the championship. Do they belong on a list of the 10 greatest basketball teams of all time? Or are championships the only true measure of greatness?

Fans must weigh many factors when choosing the greatest men's basketball teams of all time. What defines greatness to you?

LeBron James drives to the basket against the Atlanta Hawks.

NO. 10 2012–2013 MIAMI HEAT

Many call the Miami Heat of the early 2010s the first super team. In 2010, LeBron James and Chris Bosh joined Dwyane Wade in Miami. Together, they were called the Big Three. In the 2012–2013 season, the Big Three's performance would be remembered as one of the NBA's greatest seasons.

James and Wade played together in Miami for four seasons and won two NBA titles.

The Heat came out hot, going 12–3 in their first 15 games. Their offense was a threat from inside and out. They punished opponents on defense. The Heat cruised to a 66–16 regular season, the best in the NBA that year.

Miami marched through the playoffs to face the powerful San Antonio Spurs in the NBA Finals. The Heat trailed the series 3–2 before winning an overtime thriller in Game 6. Then they claimed the franchise's third NBA title with a 95–88 victory in Game 7. James scored 37 points in Game 7 and was named Finals Most Valuable Player (MVP).

2012-2013 HEAT STATS

>>> Miami won 27 games in a row from February 3 to March 25.

>>> They went 17–1 in March, becoming the first NBA team to win 17 games in a month.

>>> James led the team in scoring, averaging 26.8 points per game (PPG).

>>> Miami went 37–4 in their home games.

>>> The Heat won the Eastern Conference by 12 games over the second-place New York Knicks.

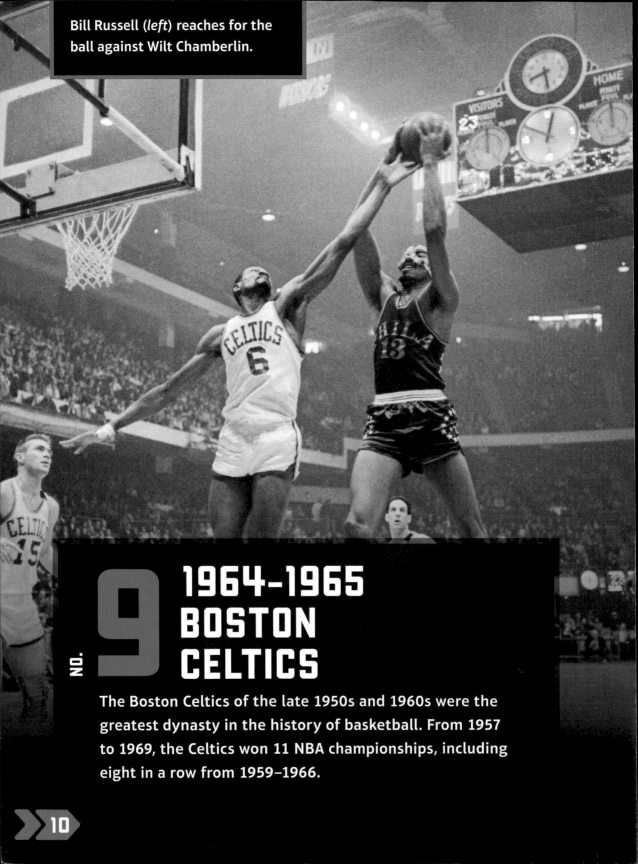

Bill Russell (*left*) reaches for the ball against Wilt Chamberlin.

NO. 9

1964-1965 BOSTON CELTICS

The Boston Celtics of the late 1950s and 1960s were the greatest dynasty in the history of basketball. From 1957 to 1969, the Celtics won 11 NBA championships, including eight in a row from 1959–1966.

Bill Russell played 13 seasons for the Celtics and averaged more than 15 PPG in his career.

The 1964–1965 Celtics were the best of the team's dynasty. The Celtics roster had five future Hall of Famers, including legendary center Bill Russell. The Celtics went 62–18, beating the second-place Cincinnati Royals by 14 games. Russell was a force, averaging 24.1 rebounds per game (RPG). Sam Jones carried the scoring load with 25.9 PPG.

The Celtics won a tight Eastern Division Finals over the Philadelphia 76ers. That set Boston up for an NBA Finals with the Los Angeles Lakers. The Celtics had no trouble beating their rivals. They locked up the title in five games and extended their amazing rule over the NBA.

1964-1965 CELTICS STATS

>>> Boston won their first 11 games of the season.

>>> They went 27–3 at home.

>>> The Celtics scored 142 points in two different games: regular season game 51 against the Baltimore Bullets and Game 1 of the NBA Finals. It was their highest point total of the season.

>>> Russell averaged 16.5 PPG and 25.2 RPG in the playoffs.

>>> The Celtics beat the Lakers 4–1 in the Finals.

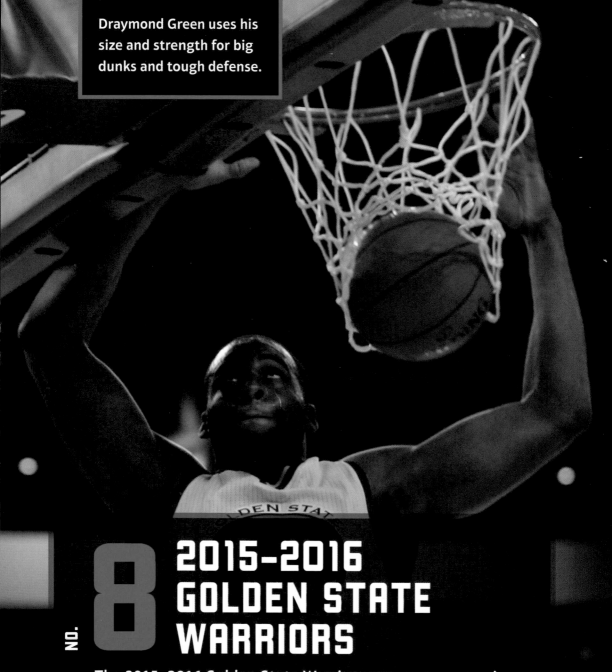

Draymond Green uses his size and strength for big dunks and tough defense.

8

2015-2016 GOLDEN STATE WARRIORS

The 2015–2016 Golden State Warriors won more games in the regular season than any team in NBA history. Guards Stephen Curry and Klay Thompson rained three-point shots. Forward Draymond Green did the dirty work near the basket. The Warriors seemed unstoppable.

Golden State opened the season 24–0. They just kept winning. The Warriors ended the regular season 73–9, the best record in NBA history.

In the NBA Finals, the Warriors were prepared to seal their place as the greatest team of all time. They led the Cleveland Cavaliers 3–1. They needed just one more win to claim the title. But the Cavs won the final three games. The Warriors finished off their amazing season without the title. They were, by far, the greatest NBA team to not win the championship.

Stephen Curry

2015–2016 WARRIORS STATS

- >>> Golden State won its first 24 games of the season. They hold the record for the longest winning streak from the start of a season.

- >>> Stephen Curry averaged 30.1 PPG and won the NBA MVP award for the second season in a row.

- >>> The Warriors never had a losing streak of more than one game

- >>> They scored more than 100 points in 19 straight games from January to March.

- >>> They averaged 114.9 PPG, the highest in the NBA that season.

Draymond Green goes up for a shot against Mason Plumlee (*center*) of the Portland Trail Blazers.

2016-2017 GOLDEN STATE WARRIORS

The 2016–2017 Warriors returned with something to prove. The year before, they had lost in the NBA Finals after winning 73 games during the regular season. After losing in the Finals, the team signed superstar Kevin Durant to join Curry, Thompson, and Green.

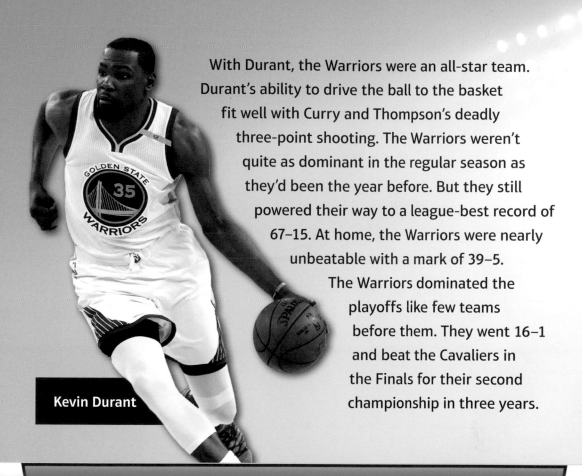

With Durant, the Warriors were an all-star team. Durant's ability to drive the ball to the basket fit well with Curry and Thompson's deadly three-point shooting. The Warriors weren't quite as dominant in the regular season as they'd been the year before. But they still powered their way to a league-best record of 67–15. At home, the Warriors were nearly unbeatable with a mark of 39–5. The Warriors dominated the playoffs like few teams before them. They went 16–1 and beat the Cavaliers in the Finals for their second championship in three years.

Kevin Durant

2016–2017 WARRIORS STATS

>>> Durant, Curry, and Thompson each averaged more than 22 PPG.

>>> The team won their games by an average of 11.6 PPG.

>>> They made 982 three-point baskets during the regular season.

>>> The Warriors won their first 15 playoff games. It earned them an NBA record for most games won in a row during the postseason.

>>> Durant averaged 28.5 PPG in the playoffs and was named the Finals MVP.

NO. 6

1999–2000 LOS ANGELES LAKERS

At the turn of the century, one of the greatest duos of all time helped revive the Los Angeles Lakers dynasty. Center Shaquille O'Neal was a force of nature down low. He bumped, banged, and overpowered his way to 29.7 PPG and earned the league MVP award.

Kobe Bryant spent his entire NBA career with the LA Lakers.

Guard Kobe Bryant was only 21 years old, but he was nearly as effective as the seasoned O'Neal. When defenses paid too much attention to O'Neal, Bryant made them pay. The Lakers had winning streaks of 16 and 19 games, helping them reach a 67–15 record. In the playoffs, they fought through the tough Western Conference to face the Indiana Pacers in the NBA Finals. The highlight of the series came when Bryant willed Los Angeles to victory in overtime of Game 4. They reclaimed their place as the NBA's greatest franchise.

1999–2000 LAKERS STATS

>>> LA had winning streaks of 19, 16, and 11 games during the regular season.

>>> Without home court advantage, the Lakers still held a record of 31–10 on the road.

>>> The Lakers came back from a 13-point deficit in Game 7 of the Western Conference Finals to beat the Portland Trail Blazers.

>>> O'Neal and Bryant led the franchise to its 12th championship.

In 1996–1997, Michael Jordan led the NBA in scoring by almost 200 points.

NO. 5

1996-1997 CHICAGO BULLS

The 1996–1997 Chicago Bulls were a well-oiled machine. The team was coming off an NBA record of 72 wins the year before. They didn't ease up on the league one bit. Michael Jordan and Scottie Pippen played lights-out offense and lockdown defense. Dennis Rodman grabbed rebounds in bunches. Toni Kukoc and Steve Kerr were sharpshooters from outside. The team piled up win after win.

Scottie Pippen hangs onto the rim after a big slam dunk.

The Bulls shined brightest in the playoffs. They faced the Utah Jazz in one of the most thrilling NBA Finals in history. The highlight came in Game 5 when Jordan played despite having the flu. He scored 38 points, earning Chicago a victory. He was so tired afterward that teammates had to help him off the court. In Game 6, Kerr neatly buried a three-pointer in the final seconds to cap off an amazing season.

1996-1997 BULLS STATS

>>> They won their first 12 games of the season and were 42–6 by the All-Star break.

>>> Pippen led the team with 5.7 assists per game.

>>> Rodman averaged 16.1 RPG.

>>> Chicago went 15–4 in the postseason to earn their fifth NBA title.

>>> Jordan averaged 31.1 PPG in the playoffs.

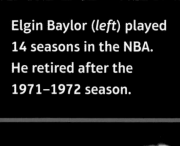

Elgin Baylor (*left*) played 14 seasons in the NBA. He retired after the 1971–1972 season.

4

1971-1972
LOS ANGELES
LAKERS

The 1971–1972 Lakers roster was loaded with game-changing talent, from Wilt Chamberlain to Jerry West to Elgin Baylor. All that star power helped make them one of the greatest teams in league history.

The Lakers were a high-flying show. They posted an NBA record for holding a winning streak of 33 games. Their 69–13 record was the best in the league.

In the playoffs, the Lakers rolled through the Chicago Bulls and Milwaukee Bucks to set up a Finals showdown with the New York Knicks. New York took Game 1 in a blowout. But then the Lakers turned it around. They won the final four games of the series to claim the championship and their place among the all-time greats.

Wilt Chamberlain

1971–1972 LAKERS STATS

> Between November 5, 1971, and January 7, 1972, the Lakers didn't lose a single game, building a record 33-game streak.

> For 24 years, the 1971–1972 Lakers held the NBA record for most games won in a single season with 69 wins.

> Both Jerry West and Gail Goodrich averaged more than 25 PPG.

> The Lakers went 12–3 in the playoffs to claim the championship.

> Head coach Bill Sharman was honored by the NBA with the Coach of the Year award.

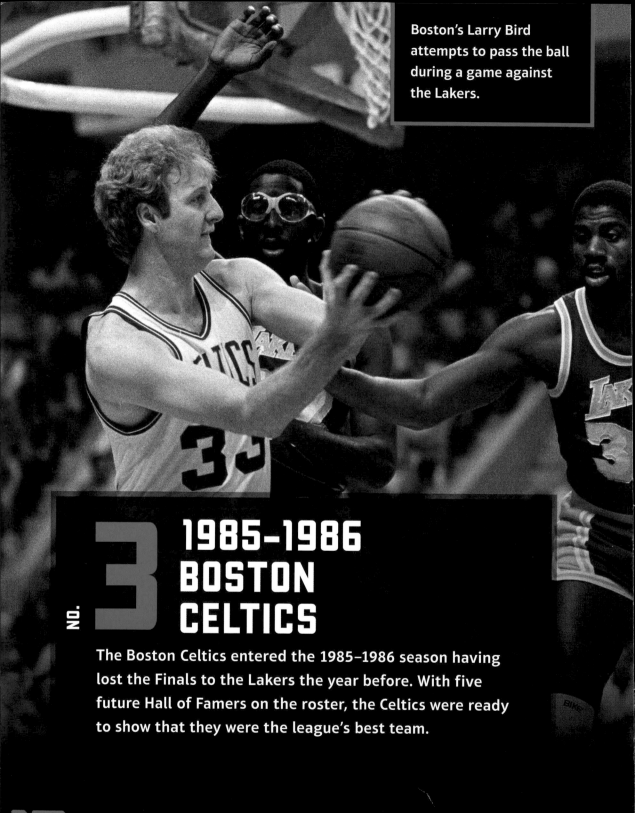

Boston's Larry Bird attempts to pass the ball during a game against the Lakers.

NO. 3

1985–1986 BOSTON CELTICS

The Boston Celtics entered the 1985–1986 season having lost the Finals to the Lakers the year before. With five future Hall of Famers on the roster, the Celtics were ready to show that they were the league's best team.

The Celtics featured a bruising defense. They allowed opponents the lowest field goal percentage in the NBA that season. The combination of slick shooting and strong defense served them well in the playoffs. Power forward Kevin McHale averaged 9.9 RPG and 24.9 PPG in the playoffs. The Celtics went 15–3 in the postseason on their way to one of the NBA's most dominant championships.

Kevin McHale

1985-1986 CELTICS STATS

>>> Larry Bird led the team with 25.8 PPG and won the league MVP award.

>>> The Celtics outscored opponents by an average of 9.4 PPG.

>>> Boston won a total of 82 games in the regular season and postseason. This earned them an NBA record for most games won in a season at the time.

>>> The team won their 16th NBA championship in 22 years.

>>> Five players averaged more than 14 PPG in the playoffs.

Michael Jordan accepts the NBA MVP award from Commissioner David Stern.

2

1995–1996 CHICAGO BULLS

In 1993, Michael Jordan left the Bulls for about a year and a half to pursue a baseball career. He returned in March 1995 to lead one of the greatest teams in NBA history. Jordan, Pippen, and rebounding machine Rodman were the cornerstones of an unstoppable team.

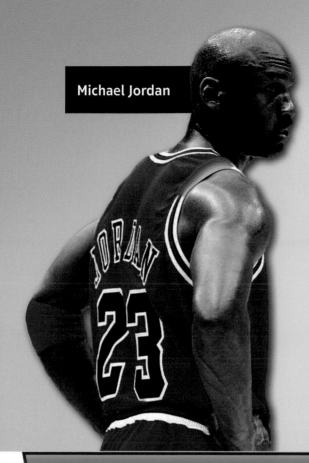

Michael Jordan

The Bulls won their first five games and never looked back. Jordan averaged a league-high 30.4 PPG in the regular season as the Bulls piled up a record 72 wins. In the playoffs, they were even better. Chicago went 11–1 in the Eastern Conference playoffs, with a single loss against the Knicks in overtime. They capped off their amazing season, defeating the Seattle SuperSonics 4–2 in the NBA Finals.

The Bulls went on to earn their second three-peat in the following two years, securing their place as one of the NBA's great dynasties.

1995–1996 BULLS STATS

>>> Rodman led the team by averaging 14.9 RPG.

>>> The Bulls outscored opponents in the regular season by an average of 12.3 PPG.

>>> From November 27, 1995, to February 2, 1996, the team went 31–1.

>>> The Bulls became the first NBA team to win 70 games, and they finished 72–10.

>>> Jordan averaged 30.7 PPG in the playoffs and was named Finals MVP.

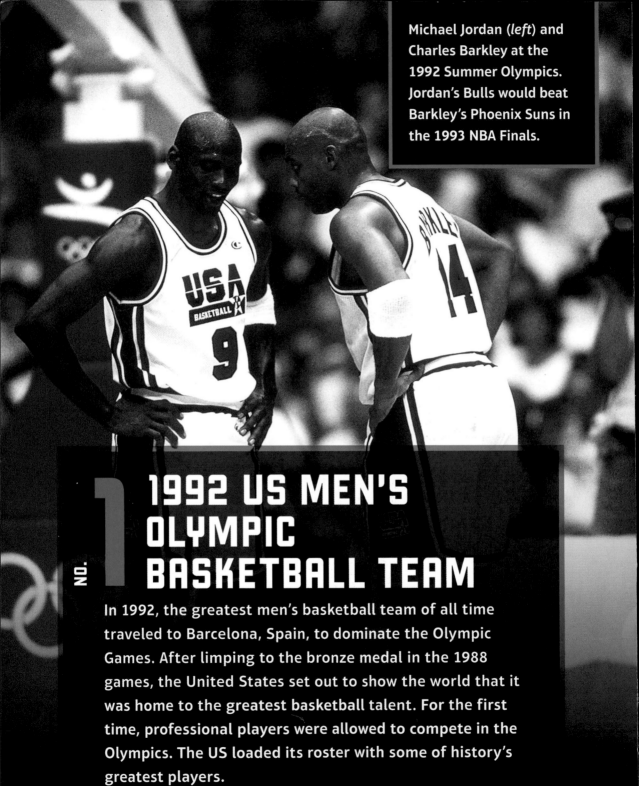

Michael Jordan (*left*) and Charles Barkley at the 1992 Summer Olympics. Jordan's Bulls would beat Barkley's Phoenix Suns in the 1993 NBA Finals.

1992 US MEN'S OLYMPIC BASKETBALL TEAM

In 1992, the greatest men's basketball team of all time traveled to Barcelona, Spain, to dominate the Olympic Games. After limping to the bronze medal in the 1988 games, the United States set out to show the world that it was home to the greatest basketball talent. For the first time, professional players were allowed to compete in the Olympics. The US loaded its roster with some of history's greatest players.

Charles Barkley (*left*) and Magic Johnson during the 1992 Olympic medal ceremony

Michael Jordan, Larry Bird, Magic Johnson, and Charles Barkley were just a few of the future Hall of Famers to lead the Dream Team. Team USA opened the Games with a 116–48 victory over Angola. That was just a taste of what followed. The Dream Team won all eight of its games by 30 points or more. They set the standard by which all other teams are measured.

1992 DREAM TEAM STATS

>>> The team included 11 Hall of Fame players.

>>> Barkley led the team in scoring with 18 PPG.

>>> The Dream Team won by an average of 43.75 PPG.

>>> Jordan was the only player to start in every game.

>>> The Dream Team also won the Tournament of the Americas, defeating Venezuela 127–80 and earning the gold medal.

YOUR G.O.A.T.

IT'S TIME TO MAKE YOUR OWN G.O.A.T. LIST.

Think about what you value most in a team. Check out the resources provided in the Learn More section of this book to help you gather information for your ranking.

What do you value most in a team? Do they need to win a championship to make the list? How important is regular-season domination? What about record-setting performances? Sort your list, and choose the greatest basketball teams of all time. Ask a friend or family member to do the same, and then compare. Where do you agree? Where do you disagree, and why? Discuss your rankings and defend your choices!

Don't stop there! What other G.O.A.T. lists can you make? How about the top 10 players or head coaches? Or the 10 greatest games of all time? Do your research, and make your lists!

BASKETBALL FACTS

>>> The first basketball game was played in 1891. The players shot at peach baskets and had to retrieve the ball from the basket after every score.

>>> The Boston Celtics, with 17 titles, have the most NBA championships. The Lakers are close behind with 16. No other team has more than six.

>>> On December 13, 1983, the Detroit Pistons beat the Denver Nuggets 186–184. Their 370 combined points is the most ever in a single game.

>>> The longest game in NBA history happened on January 6, 1951. The Indianapolis Olympians beat the Rochester Royals in six overtimes.

>>> Kareem Abdul-Jabbar holds the NBA record for most career points with 38,387. Wilt Chamberlain holds the record for most points in a single game with 100.

GLOSSARY

blowout: a game in which one team wins by a wide margin

clutch: a high-pressure situation, often late in a game or in the playoffs

dynasty: a long period of dominance by a team, usually including multiple championships

field goal: any basketball shot that is not a free throw

franchise: the entire organization of a team that is part of a large league

overtime: five-minute periods played after a tie game at the end of regular play to decide a winner

professional: someone who makes a living by playing a sport

rebound: to gain possession of the ball after a missed shot

rival: a team or player with whom one has especially intense competition

three-peat: three consecutive championships

LEARN MORE

Basketball Reference
https://www.basketball-reference.com/

Gilliam, Mickey. *Pro Basketball Upsets*. Minneapolis: Lerner Publications, 2020.

Levit, Joe. *Basketball's G.O.A.T.: Michael Jordan, LeBron James, and More*. Minneapolis: Lerner Publications, 2020.

The Official Site of the NBA
https://www.nba.com/

Sports Illustrated Kids: Basketball
https://www.sikids.com/basketball

Weakland, Mark. *Basketball Records*. Mankato, MN: Black Rabbit Books, 2021.

INDEX

PHOTO ACKNOWLEDGMENTS

Image credits: EFKS/Shutterstock.com, pp. 2-3, 28-29, 30-31; Jonathan Daniel/ Getty Images, p. 4; ESB Professional/Shutterstock.com, p. 5 (background throughout); Jared Wickerham/Getty Images, p. 6; Nuccio DiNuzzo/Chicago Tribune/Tribune News Service/Getty Images, p. 7; Mike Ehrmann/Getty Images, p. 8; Ronald Martinez/Getty Images, p. 9; Bettmann/Getty Images, pp. 10, 20, 22 AP Photo, p. 11; AP Photo/Marcio Jose Sanchez, p. 12; Thearon W. Henderson/ Getty Images, p. 13; Ezra Shaw/Getty Images, pp. 14, 15; Mike Nelson/AFP/Getty Images, p. 16; ince Bucci/AFP/Getty Images, p. 17; AP Photo/Tom DiPace, p. 18; AP Photo/Rick Bowmer, p. 19; Focus on Sport/Getty Images, p. 21; Jim Wilson/The Boston Globe/Getty Images, p. 23; Photo by Sporting News/Getty Images, p. 24; JEFF HAYNES/AFP/Getty Images, p. 25; Icon Sportswire/Getty Images, pp. 26, 27; Pongnathee Kluaythong/EyeEm/Getty Images, p. 28 (insert).

Cover: Jonathan Ferrey/Getty Images.